WHY YOU'RE
THE BEST TEACHER
EVER

My favorite thing about you is

_____.

2

You are the best at

_____.

You make learning stuff fun, even

_____ .

4

You taught me to

_____.

5

You deserve the Best

Award.

I like how you always make us

——————————————————————————— .

I like how you never make us

——————————————————————————.

It makes me feel really good when

_____.

Nobody else can

———————————————————————

like you.

10

You give the best lessons on

_____.

11

You're so patient when

_____.

12

If you were a superhero,
your superpower would be

_____.

13

You inspire me to

_____ .

14

I hope everyone appreciates how

_____

you are.

15

It totally rocks when you

_____ .

16

I like that you encourage me to

_____.

17

I always want to hear what
you're going to say about

_____.

18

The way you explained

———————————————————

was just the best.

It makes me smile when you

_____.

20

The best thing about
our classroom is

_____.

21

You always help me

_____ .

22

I hope you get to

_____

this summer.

23

I admire you for

_____.

24

I like it when you say

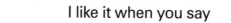.

25

You deserve a lifetime supply of

_____.

26

If I had to describe you
in one word, it'd be

_____.

27

Your

_____

is my favorite.

28

Thanks for putting up with my

_____.

29

You give the best advice on

_____.

30

I like the way you let us talk about

_____.

31

I wish more people could

_____

your

_____.

32

You are the best

I've ever known.

33

Thanks for listening when I

_____ .

34

It's super cool how you

_____.

35

I never knew

_____

until your class.

36

I'd like to know how you

_____ .

37

I am so

_____

that

_____.

38

I like it best when you

_____ .

39

You made us all crack up when you

_____.

40

I hope to be as

_____

as you one day.

41

You were totally right about

_____.

42

You're really good at

_____.

43

The best thing we've done in class is

_____.

44

It means so much that
you showed me how to

_____.

45

You cheer me up when

_____ .

That time you

_____

was so funny!

47

You make our school a more

_____

place.

48

If I could grant you one wish it'd be

_____.

49

Thank you for

_____.

50

The best thing I learned from you is

_____.

YOU'RE THE BEST TEACHER EVER!

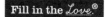

Created, published, and distributed by Knock Knock
6080 Center Drive
Los Angeles, CA 90045
knockknockstuff.com
Knock Knock is a registered trademark of Knock Knock LLC
Fill in the Love is a registered trademark of Knock Knock LLC

ISBN: 978-168349001-2
UPC: 825703-50256-5
10 9 8 7 6

#fillinthelove